From Startup to Success
The Entrepreneur's
"Guide"

Index

Part I
Planting the Seed - Nurturing Your Business Idea

Idea Generation: At the heart of every successful business lies a groundbreaking idea. Just as a seed holds the potential for a majestic tree, an innovative concept has the power to evolve into a thriving venture. Idea generation is the pivotal starting point, where entrepreneurs identify gaps in the market or envision solutions to unmet needs. This phase is characterized by brainstorming, research, and creative exploration, leading to the formulation of an idea that holds promise for transformation.

Business Planning: With the seed of an idea in hand, entrepreneurs begin crafting the blueprint for their venture. Business planning involves converting concepts into concrete strategies. This stage lays out the company's mission, vision, goals, and the practical steps to achieve them. Comprehensive planning also includes identifying target demographics, understanding market trends, and projecting potential revenue streams. A well-structured plan is like a roadmap guiding the startup's growth trajectory.

Research and Validation: Before sowing the seed, it's crucial to ensure that the soil is fertile. Similarly, before launching a startup, entrepreneurs engage in extensive research and validation. This process involves delving into market dynamics, consumer preferences, and competitor landscapes. By seeking validation through surveys, focus groups, or even pilot projects, entrepreneurs gain valuable insights that help refine their offerings and mitigate risks.

Building the Team: Just as a tree thrives when its roots are strong, a startup's foundation is built upon a skilled and passionate team. Entrepreneurs seek out individuals who complement their strengths and contribute expertise to various aspects of the business. Building the right team fosters synergy, collective creativity, and shared commitment toward realizing the startup's vision.

Securing Funding: A seed requires nourishment to grow, and a startup requires financial support to take root. Securing funding is a critical step in bringing an idea to fruition. Entrepreneurs explore diverse funding avenues, from personal savings and loans to seeking investments from angel investors or venture capitalists. Adequate funding provides the resources necessary for initial development, marketing, and operations.

Creating the Brand: Much like the leaves and blossoms of a tree, a brand identity distinguishes a startup in a crowded marketplace. Entrepreneurs create a unique brand that resonates with their target audience. This encompasses designing a captivating logo, defining the brand's personality, and crafting a consistent narrative. A compelling brand identity establishes an emotional connection with customers and communicates the startup's essence.

Initial Execution: With all preparations in place, it's time to plant the seed and witness the first shoots of growth. Initial execution involves translating plans into action. Whether it's developing a prototype, crafting a minimum viable product, or offering pilot services, this phase marks the tangible beginning of the entrepreneurial journey. By embracing experimentation, iteration, and adaptability, entrepreneurs navigate this phase with the aim of nurturing their seedling startup toward future success.

Just as the growth of a tree is influenced by factors like sunlight, water, and nutrients, the growth of a startup is influenced by strategic planning, market insights, teamwork, and the ability to adapt to changing circumstances. By nurturing each aspect of "Planting the Seed," entrepreneurs create a strong foundation for their business to flourish.

"Entrepreneurship is like planting a seed in fertile ground. With a visionary idea as the seed, strategic planning as the soil, and dedicated effort as the water, it grows into a remarkable journey of growth and transformation."
"Navigating Uncertainty: Overcoming Idea Viability Challenges"

1. Problem: Uncertainty in Idea Viability

   - Answer: Thorough market research and validation through surveys or focus groups can help gauge the demand and potential success of the idea.

2. Problem: Lack of Clear Business Plan

   - Answer: Develop a comprehensive business plan that outlines your goals, strategies, target market, and financial projections. This plan serves as a roadmap for your venture.

3. Problem: Difficulty in Securing Funding

   - Answer: Explore various funding options, such as personal savings, angel investors, venture capital, or crowdfunding. A solid business plan and a compelling pitch can attract investors.

4. Problem: Ineffective Team Building

   - Answer: Carefully select team members based on their skills, experience, and alignment with the startup's vision. Strong communication and shared values are key to a cohesive team.

5. Problem: Market Validation Challenges

   - Answer: Conduct thorough market research to understand customer needs, preferences, and pain points. Test your product or service with a small audience before full launch.

6. Problem: Competition and Differentiation

- Answer: Differentiate your startup by offering unique value, exceptional quality, or innovative features. Communicate your distinctiveness clearly in your branding.

7. Problem: Legal and Regulatory Hurdles

   - Answer: Research the legal requirements for your industry and location. Register your business, obtain necessary licenses, and ensure compliance with regulations.

8. Problem: Limited Initial Resources

   - Answer: Start small and focus on the essentials. Prioritize tasks, allocate resources wisely, and consider lean strategies to maximize efficiency.

9. Problem: Scaling Challenges

   - Answer: Plan for scalability from the beginning. Implement systems and processes that can accommodate growth, and continually assess and adapt as you expand.

10. Problem: Fear of Failure

    - Answer: Embrace failure as a learning experience. Each setback provides valuable insights that contribute to the refinement and success of your venture.

Navigating these challenges requires a combination of research, resilience, adaptability, and proactive problem-solving. By acknowledging potential obstacles and having strategies in place to address them, entrepreneurs can better prepare themselves for the journey of planting the seed and growing their startups successfully.

The Entrepreneurial Spirit:

Embracing the Journey Ahead

At the core of every successful startup lies the unwavering force known as the entrepreneurial spirit. It embodies the courage to forge new paths, the determination to overcome challenges, and the unrelenting passion to turn innovative ideas into tangible reality. This chapter delves into the essence of the entrepreneurial spirit and how it acts as the driving force that propels individuals toward embracing the journey of entrepreneurship with enthusiasm and resilience.

The entrepreneurial spirit is not merely a concept; it's a mindset that fuels transformation. Entrepreneurs possess a unique ability to see opportunities where others might see obstacles. They envision a world that could be, rather than one that already exists. This chapter explores the mindset shift required to foster this spirit, highlighting the importance of embracing uncertainty, taking calculated risks, and being open to failure as a stepping stone toward success. It emphasizes the significance of audacity, encouraging readers to break free from the comfort zone and embrace the uncharted territory of their business ventures.

Moreover, the chapter dives into the role of self-belief in nurturing the entrepreneurial spirit. It discusses how a resolute belief in one's vision becomes the cornerstone of all entrepreneurial endeavors. Entrepreneurs must not only believe in their idea but also in their ability to bring it to fruition. The narrative underscores the power of conviction and the ability to rally support around a shared goal, fostering an environment where innovation thrives and the entrepreneurial spirit can flourish.

Ultimately, this chapter serves as a foundational guide for aspiring entrepreneurs, shedding light on the intangible but vital aspects of the entrepreneurial journey. It instills in readers the significance of cultivating an unwavering entrepreneurial spirit, emphasizing that with the right mindset, one can embark on the path to creating impactful change, bringing visionary ideas to life, and leaving an indelible mark on the world of business and beyond.

Key questions

Question 1: What are some key traits that define the entrepreneurial spirit?

Answer: Traits such as resilience, creativity, risk-taking, adaptability, and a willingness to embrace uncertainty characterize the entrepreneurial spirit.

Question 2: Can the entrepreneurial spirit be nurtured and developed over time?

Answer: Yes, the entrepreneurial spirit can be cultivated through experience, learning, and exposure to new challenges. Surrounding oneself with supportive mentors and like-minded individuals can aid in its development.

Question 3: How does the entrepreneurial spirit contribute to personal growth?

Answer: The entrepreneurial spirit encourages individuals to step out of their comfort zones, face challenges head-on, and learn from failures, leading to personal growth and increased self-confidence.

Question 4: What are some potential downsides of excessive risk-taking associated with the entrepreneurial spirit?

Answer: While risk-taking is a key aspect of entrepreneurship, excessive risk without proper analysis can lead to failure, financial loss, and damage to one's reputation.

Question 5: How can entrepreneurs maintain their entrepreneurial spirit during times of adversity?

Answer: Staying focused on the vision, seeking support from mentors and peers, and viewing challenges as learning opportunities can help entrepreneurs persevere through tough times.

The Power of Vision
Turning Dreams into Reality

In the landscape of entrepreneurship, the power of vision stands as the compass guiding entrepreneurs through the tumultuous seas of challenges and opportunities. This chapter delves into the profound impact of having a clear and compelling vision and how it serves as the cornerstone for transforming dreams into tangible realities in the business world.

A vision is more than just a lofty goal; it's a vivid and inspiring picture of what an entrepreneur aims to achieve. It acts as a north star, providing direction, purpose, and motivation to every action taken. This chapter explores the process of crafting a vision that not only ignites passion within the entrepreneur but also resonates with team members, investors, and customers. It underscores the importance of a vision that encapsulates not just the "what," but also the "why" and "how," fostering a sense of shared purpose and commitment.

Furthermore, the chapter delves into the transformative role of a well-defined vision in decision-making. It discusses how a strong vision provides a framework for evaluating opportunities, ensuring that each step taken aligns with the ultimate destination. This ability to focus on the big picture while navigating the minutiae of daily operations is a hallmark of visionary entrepreneurs. The narrative emphasizes the need for adaptability within the vision, allowing it to evolve alongside changing market dynamics and the growth of the business.

The chapter also highlights the inspirational aspect of a vision, both for the entrepreneur and those involved in the venture. It explores how a compelling vision can inspire creativity, foster resilience, and drive innovation. By offering a glimpse into a better future, the vision serves as a rallying point, uniting teams and stakeholders toward a shared goal that transcends short-term challenges.

Ultimately, this chapter guides readers in harnessing the power of vision as a transformative force in their entrepreneurial journey. It underscores that a vision is not a static declaration but a dynamic force that propels entrepreneurs forward, infusing their actions with purpose, resilience, and the determination to turn dreams into tangible successes.

Key questions

Question 1: What role does a clear vision play in the success of a business?

Answer: A clear vision acts as a guiding force, inspiring and aligning team members, helping prioritize goals, and providing a framework for decision-making.

Question 2: Can a vision be too broad or too narrow?

Answer: Yes, a vision that is too broad may lack focus, while a vision that is too narrow may limit growth opportunities. A balanced vision is specific enough to guide actions but flexible enough to adapt.

Question 3: How can an entrepreneur effectively communicate their vision to their team?

Answer: Effective communication involves storytelling, using visual aids, and engaging in open dialogues that help team members understand the "why" behind the vision.

Question 4: What strategies can entrepreneurs use to keep their vision relevant as their business evolves?
Answer: Regularly reviewing and adjusting the vision to incorporate changing market dynamics and new insights ensures that it remains relevant and inspiring.
Question 5: Can a strong vision attract investors and stakeholders to a business?
Answer: Yes, a compelling vision can generate enthusiasm among investors and stakeholders who see the potential for growth and positive impact.

Defying Limits
Aiming High in the Business World

In the realm of business, those who dare to defy limits are the ones who reshape industries, rewrite success stories, and leave an indelible mark on the world. This chapter delves into the art of aiming high, pushing boundaries, and embracing the mindset that challenges can be opportunities in disguise.

Entrepreneurs who choose to defy limits refuse to be confined by conventional norms or perceived constraints. Instead, they see limitations as mere stepping stones on the path to greatness. This chapter explores how adopting this audacious mindset opens doors to unexplored avenues, encouraging entrepreneurs to take calculated risks and pursue ambitions that others might consider unattainable. It underscores the notion that achieving greatness demands stepping out of comfort zones and embracing the exhilarating uncertainty of uncharted territory.

Moreover, the chapter delves into the role of perseverance in defying limits. The road to success is rarely smooth, and challenges are an inevitable part of the journey. Entrepreneurs who aim high understand that obstacles are not roadblocks but opportunities to innovate, pivot, and grow. It discusses strategies to cultivate resilience, emphasizing the importance of viewing setbacks as temporary setbacks rather than permanent failures. This mindset shift fuels the determination to overcome challenges and turn adversity into an advantage.

The narrative also delves into the influence of a daring vision on inspiring others to join the journey. Entrepreneurs who aim high not only inspire their teams but also attract investors, partners, and customers who are drawn to their audacity. By challenging the status quo, these visionary leaders create a movement that sparks enthusiasm and drives change. This chapter encourages readers to lead by example and set the pace for the kind of ambition that not only transforms their businesses but also leaves a lasting legacy. Ultimately, this chapter serves as a catalyst for embracing audacious aspirations and believing in the possibility of achieving what might seem impossible. It inspires entrepreneurs to break free from self-imposed limitations, confront challenges head-on, and redefine success on their terms. By defying limits, entrepreneurs set in motion a journey that doesn't just lead to business achievements, but to an enduring impact on industries, communities, and the world.

Key questions

Question 1: Why is it important for entrepreneurs to push beyond their comfort zones?

Answer: Pushing beyond comfort zones fosters growth, drives innovation, and exposes entrepreneurs to new challenges that can lead to valuable learning experiences.

Question 2: How can entrepreneurs balance the pursuit of ambitious goals with the need for practicality?

Answer: By breaking down ambitious goals into smaller, achievable steps and carefully evaluating the risks and resources required, entrepreneurs can strike a balance between ambition and practicality.

Question 3: What role does failure play in defying limits and achieving success?

Answer: Failure is often a stepping stone to success. Embracing failure as a learning opportunity enables entrepreneurs to refine strategies and make informed decisions that ultimately lead to breakthroughs.

Question 4: How can entrepreneurs foster a growth mindset within their teams?

Answer: Encourage a culture where experimentation is valued, provide constructive feedback, celebrate both successes and failures, and offer opportunities for skill development.

Question 5: Can defying limits lead to burnout or unsustainable practices?

Answer: Yes, pushing too hard without proper planning or work-life balance can lead to burnout. It's important to manage energy levels and maintain a healthy approach to growth.

Remember, starting a business requires thorough research, careful planning, and a willingness to adapt. While these answers provide a starting point, seeking advice from mentors, consulting experts, and networking within your industry can provide more personalized insights and guidance.

The Idea That Sparks Change

Identifying a Niche

In the boundless landscape of entrepreneurship, success often hinges on a singular idea—an idea that not only captures the imagination but also possesses the potential to revolutionize industries and spark transformative change. This chapter delves into the art of identifying that pivotal idea, the beacon that guides entrepreneurs toward carving their distinct path in the business world.

The process of identifying a niche involves a delicate balance between innovation and market demand. Entrepreneurs embark on a journey of exploration, seeking gaps and unmet needs within existing markets. It's about uncovering opportunities that might be overlooked by larger players, and envisioning solutions that cater to specific, often underserved, segments of the population. This chapter underscores that finding the right niche is not just about inventing something new; it's about understanding the unique value that your idea brings to the table.

Moreover, the narrative highlights the critical role of passion and personal resonance in identifying a niche. True innovation often emerges from a genuine passion for solving a problem or making a difference. Entrepreneurs find themselves drawn to ideas that resonate with their own experiences, expertise, and aspirations. This chapter encourages readers to tap into their own passions and life experiences, as these can be wellsprings of inspiration for creating something that is both meaningful and commercially viable. In the world of business, identifying a niche isn't merely about carving a niche for oneself; it's about creating an ecosystem of change. A well-chosen niche can disrupt existing norms, challenge the status quo, and lead to innovations that shape the future. This chapter imparts the message that in the pursuit of an idea that sparks change, entrepreneurs must be prepared to embrace risk, uncertainty, and the possibility of failure. It's a journey that requires a blend of creativity, strategic thinking, and a willingness to relentlessly pursue excellence.

"Entrepreneurship is about identifying a gap in the world and daring to fill it. The power to spark change lies in the courage to embrace uncharted territory and transform an idea into a tangible force of innovation."

Question 1: What is the significance of identifying a niche market?

Answer: Identifying a niche allows entrepreneurs to serve a specific audience with unique needs, enabling them to differentiate themselves in a crowded market.

Question 2: How can entrepreneurs validate that their chosen niche is viable?

Answer: Validating a niche involves conducting market research, seeking feedback from potential customers, and ensuring that there is genuine demand for the product or service.

Question 3: Can an entrepreneur pivot their niche if the initial one isn't successful?

Answer: Yes, entrepreneurs can pivot their niche if they identify a better opportunity or if the current niche isn't generating the desired results. Flexibility is key.

Question 4: Is it possible to combine multiple niches within a single business?

Answer: Yes, a business can cater to multiple niches, especially if they share common needs or interests. However, maintaining focus and consistency is important to avoid dilution.

Question 5: What advantages can come from serving a niche market over a broader audience?

Answer: Serving a niche allows for more targeted marketing, greater customer loyalty, reduced competition, and the opportunity to establish a strong brand identity.

Crafting Your Blueprint
Writing an Effective Business Plan

Every successful endeavor begins with a meticulously crafted blueprint, a plan that outlines the journey ahead and serves as a guiding compass through uncharted waters. In the realm of entrepreneurship, this guiding blueprint takes the form of a business plan—a comprehensive document that crystallizes the vision, strategies, and operational intricacies of a startup. This chapter delves into the significance of crafting a well-structured business plan and how it lays the foundation for turning aspirations into reality.

At its core, a business plan is a roadmap that navigates entrepreneurs through the complexities of startup development. It's a strategic document that provides a clear roadmap, outlining goals, target markets, competitive analysis, marketing strategies, and financial projections. This chapter underscores the essential elements of an effective business plan, emphasizing the need for succinct yet comprehensive articulation of every facet of the startup's journey.

The act of writing a business plan is more than just documenting ideas; it's a process of refining concepts and establishing a cohesive vision. This chapter delves into the role of business planning in identifying potential pitfalls and developing contingency strategies. It empowers entrepreneurs to critically assess their assumptions, recognize potential challenges, and outline proactive measures to overcome obstacles.

Furthermore, the narrative highlights the multifaceted uses of a well-crafted business plan. It serves as a tool for attracting investors, convincing stakeholders, and guiding day-to-day operations. This chapter advocates for a dynamic approach to business planning—one that acknowledges the fluid nature of startups and the need to adapt and pivot as circumstances evolve.

In the end, crafting a business plan is an exercise in both strategy and communication. It's an opportunity for entrepreneurs to articulate their vision with clarity and conviction, bridging the gap between an idea's conception and its realization. This chapter encourages readers to approach business planning as an iterative process, one that evolves as the startup progresses. Just as a blueprint guides the construction of a magnificent structure, a well-crafted business plan paves the way for the construction of a successful business venture.

Question 1: What is the purpose of a business plan in the entrepreneurial journey?

Answer: A business plan serves as a roadmap that outlines your business's goals, strategies, target market, competition, financial projections, and operational details. It provides a comprehensive guide for executing your business idea.

Question 2: What key components should be included in a business plan?

Answer: A business plan typically includes an executive summary, company description, market analysis, organization structure, product/service description, marketing strategy, financial projections, and an implementation timeline.

Question 3: How does a well-crafted business plan help entrepreneurs secure funding?

Answer: A well-structured business plan demonstrates to potential investors or lenders that the entrepreneur has thoroughly analyzed the market, understands the business's financial needs, and has a clear strategy for achieving success.

Question 4: Can a business plan be a flexible document that evolves over time?

Answer: Yes, a business plan should be adaptable as the business grows and the market changes. Regularly reviewing and updating the plan helps keep it aligned with current realities and goals.

Question 5: What are the common pitfalls to avoid when creating a business plan?

Answer: Avoid over-optimistic projections, lack of market research, neglecting competition analysis, and writing a plan that's too lengthy or complex. A clear and concise plan is more effective.

Part II
Cultivating Growth Overcoming Challenges and Expanding

Overcoming Doubts
Cultivating a Resilient Mindset

In the landscape of entrepreneurship, doubts are the shadows that accompany every step of the journey. However, it's not the presence of doubt that defines success, but rather how entrepreneurs confront and conquer it. This chapter delves into the art of cultivating a resilient mindset—one that thrives in the face of uncertainty, embraces failure as a stepping stone, and turns doubts into catalysts for growth.

A resilient mindset is the bedrock upon which successful entrepreneurs build their ventures. It's a mental framework that acknowledges challenges as integral to the journey and views setbacks as opportunities to learn and adapt. This chapter underscores that resilience is not an inherent trait but a skill that can be cultivated through self-awareness, practice, and a commitment to personal growth.

The narrative explores strategies for overcoming doubts and developing mental fortitude. It delves into the importance of self-belief and the impact of positive affirmations in navigating the unpredictable terrain of entrepreneurship. This chapter advocates for seeking inspiration from those who have overcome adversities, highlighting the transformative stories of successful entrepreneurs who turned doubts into the fuel for their endeavors.

Moreover, the chapter emphasizes the role of failure in the entrepreneurial narrative. Resilience lies not in avoiding failure, but in learning from it. Entrepreneurs are encouraged to reframe failure as a valuable learning experience, fostering the ability to bounce back stronger and wiser. By embracing a growth mindset, entrepreneurs transform doubts from hindrances into stepping stones on the path to success.

"In the realm of entrepreneurship, doubt is the canvas upon which resilience paints its masterpiece. Embrace doubt not as an obstacle, but as a brush that adds texture and depth to your journey."

Question 1: How can entrepreneurs overcome self-doubt and maintain a resilient mindset?

Answer: Practicing self-awareness, focusing on strengths, seeking support from mentors, and reframing failures as learning experiences can help entrepreneurs overcome doubts and build resilience.

Question 2: How does a resilient mindset impact decision-making during challenging times?

Answer: A resilient mindset enables entrepreneurs to make decisions based on rational analysis rather than fear, helping them navigate challenges more effectively and make informed choices.

Question 3: Can resilience be learned, or is it an inherent trait?

Answer: Resilience can be learned and developed over time through experience, introspection, and a willingness to adapt and learn from setbacks.

Question 4: What strategies can entrepreneurs use to bounce back from failures?

Answer: Entrepreneurs can bounce back by embracing failure as a stepping stone, analyzing mistakes without blame, seeking feedback, and maintaining a forward-focused attitude.

Question 5: How can entrepreneurs foster resilience within their teams?

Answer: Encouraging open communication, recognizing and celebrating small victories, providing opportunities for skill development, and offering psychological support can help build resilience within teams.

"The secret of getting ahead is getting started." - Mark Twain

Building Blocks
Strategies for a Strong Start

In the intricate tapestry of entrepreneurship, the foundation of a startup resembles a mosaic of carefully positioned building blocks. Just as a sturdy structure relies on the stability of its foundational elements, a successful business venture hinges on the strategic implementation of foundational strategies. This chapter delves into the vital importance of these "building blocks" and explores the key strategies that lay the groundwork for a robust and resilient startup launch.

The journey of a startup begins with the meticulous arrangement of its foundational building blocks. These building blocks encompass various aspects, including market research, target audience identification, product or service development, branding, and marketing strategies. By attending to each block with precision, entrepreneurs create a solid base upon which the entire venture rests.

This chapter delves into the significance of market research as an essential building block. Thorough research equips entrepreneurs with insights into market trends, customer preferences, and potential competitors. Armed with this knowledge, they can tailor their offerings to meet the needs of their target audience, ensuring a strong market fit.

Another critical building block is the development of a unique value proposition (UVP). This chapter explores strategies for crafting a UVP that sets the startup apart from competitors and communicates its distinctive benefits to potential customers. By defining what makes the venture exceptional, entrepreneurs lay the groundwork for effective branding and positioning.

Furthermore, this chapter delves into the role of branding as a building block for recognition and credibility. A compelling brand identity cultivates an emotional connection with customers, fostering trust and loyalty. Strategies for creating a consistent and compelling brand presence are explored in depth.

In tandem with branding, marketing strategies form another integral building block. From social media campaigns to content marketing and beyond, effective marketing strategies help entrepreneurs connect with their target audience and generate interest in their offerings. The chapter highlights the importance of tailoring marketing approaches to the preferences and behaviors of the intended customer base.

In conclusion, the art of launching a startup rests upon the careful assembly of building blocks that contribute to its strength and stability. Just as each block fits into place to create a harmonious structure, each strategic decision in entrepreneurship contributes to the startup's overall viability. By meticulously considering the foundational elements of market research, value proposition, branding, and marketing, entrepreneurs pave the way for a strong and impactful startup launch.

Question 1: What are the key components of a strong business foundation?
Answer: A strong foundation includes a clear business plan, market analysis, a viable value proposition, a solid marketing strategy, operational processes, and a clear understanding of the target audience.

Question 2: Why is market research crucial when establishing a business?
Answer: Market research provides insights into customer needs, preferences, and competition, enabling entrepreneurs to tailor their offerings and strategies for success.

Question 3: How can entrepreneurs differentiate themselves in a competitive market?
Answer: Entrepreneurs can differentiate by offering unique value, providing exceptional customer service, leveraging innovative technology, and consistently delivering on promises.

Question 4: What role does adaptability play in the early stages of a business?
Answer: Adaptability allows businesses to respond to changing market conditions and customer feedback, helping them refine their strategies and stay relevant.

Question 5: How can entrepreneurs strike a balance between innovation and stability during the startup phase?
Answer: Entrepreneurs can innovate while ensuring that core processes and customer satisfaction remain stable. Gradual experimentation helps maintain equilibrium.

"Great things are not done by impulse, but by a series of small things brought together." - Vincent van Gogh

"The entrepreneur always searches for change, responds to it, and exploits it as an opportunity." - Peter Drucker

The Right Team

Assembling a Cohesive and Committed Staff

In the intricate ecosystem of entrepreneurship, a startup's success is often woven from the collaborative efforts of a dedicated team. Just as a symphony requires the harmonious interplay of various instruments, a thriving business venture relies on the synchronization of individuals who bring diverse skills and shared commitment to the table. This chapter delves into the significance of assembling the right team and explores strategies for creating a cohesive and committed staff that propels the startup toward its goals.

A startup's team is more than the sum of its parts; it's the lifeblood that fuels innovation, resilience, and growth. This chapter underscores the pivotal role of team dynamics in shaping the venture's trajectory. It emphasizes that the journey is not one to be embarked upon alone but rather with individuals who share the entrepreneurial vision and contribute unique strengths.

Entrepreneurs are tasked with the challenge of assembling a team that complements their expertise and contributes a diverse range of skills. This chapter explores strategies for identifying team members whose strengths align with the startup's needs, creating a synergy that fosters creative problem-solving and mutual support.

Cohesion within the team is essential for effective collaboration. The narrative delves into strategies for nurturing a culture of open communication, mutual respect, and shared goals. By fostering an environment where team members feel valued and heard, entrepreneurs lay the foundation for a collaborative work culture that breeds success.

Furthermore, commitment is the glue that holds a team together through challenges and triumphs. This chapter discusses the importance of aligning team members with the startup's vision and values, fostering a sense of purpose that transcends individual tasks. Strategies for inspiring dedication and motivation are explored, emphasizing the significance of leadership that leads by example.

In conclusion, the right team is not merely a collection of individuals but a constellation of stars that illuminate the path of entrepreneurial success. Assembling a cohesive and committed staff requires careful consideration, a discerning eye for talent, and the nurturing of a positive work culture. By investing in the strength and unity of the team, entrepreneurs set the stage for a venture that not only survives but thrives.

Question 1: Why is building the right team crucial for a successful business?

Answer: The right team brings diverse skills, perspectives, and strengths, contributing to effective decision-making, creativity, and the ability to execute strategies.

Question 2: What qualities should entrepreneurs look for when hiring team members?
Answer: Entrepreneurs should seek individuals with relevant skills, cultural fit, a growth mindset, strong communication, and a willingness to collaborate.
Question 3: How can entrepreneurs ensure that their team remains motivated and committed?
Answer: Recognize and reward achievements, provide opportunities for professional development, foster open communication, and create a positive work environment that values input.
Question 4: What strategies can entrepreneurs employ to manage conflicts within their team?
Answer: Encourage open dialogue, establish clear expectations, address conflicts promptly, and focus on finding mutually beneficial solutions to maintain team cohesion.
Question 5: Can a diverse team enhance innovation and problem-solving within a business?
Answer: Yes, diverse teams bring different perspectives and experiences, fostering innovative thinking and enabling a more comprehensive approach to solving challenges.
"Individual commitment to a group effort—that is what makes a team work, a company work, a society work, a civilization work." - Vince Lombardi
"Teamwork makes the dream work." - John C. Maxwell

Funding Your Vision
Exploring Funding Options

In the dynamic landscape of entrepreneurship, transforming a visionary idea into a tangible reality often requires a critical ingredient: funding. Just as seeds need nourishment to grow into thriving plants, startups need financial support to flourish and reach their full potential. This chapter delves into the diverse funding options available to entrepreneurs and explores the strategies for navigating this critical aspect of the entrepreneurial journey. Securing funding is a pivotal phase that can make or break a startup's trajectory. This chapter highlights the significance of aligning financial resources with the startup's growth plans, emphasizing that the right funding strategy can provide the necessary fuel for innovation, development, and market expansion. Entrepreneurs face a multitude of funding options, each with its own merits and considerations. This chapter provides insights into various avenues, including personal savings, angel investors, venture capital, bank loans, crowdfunding, and grants. It discusses the criteria, benefits, and potential drawbacks of each option, helping entrepreneurs make informed decisions based on their startup's unique needs and goals.

Strategies for crafting a compelling pitch are also explored. Whether presenting to angel investors, venture capitalists, or potential backers on crowdfunding platforms, entrepreneurs must effectively communicate their vision, market potential, and competitive advantage. This chapter offers guidance on tailoring pitches to resonate with different types of investors.

Furthermore, the narrative delves into the importance of financial planning and prudent resource allocation. Entrepreneurs are encouraged to create realistic budgets that reflect their startup's growth trajectory. By demonstrating a thorough understanding of financial needs and projections, entrepreneurs enhance their credibility and attractiveness to potential investors.

In conclusion, funding a startup is a strategic dance that requires careful consideration, research, and a comprehensive understanding of available options. By exploring various funding avenues, honing their pitch, and ensuring sound financial planning, entrepreneurs can bring their visionary ideas to life and set their ventures on a trajectory of growth and success.

Question 1: What are some common funding options available to entrepreneurs?

Answer: Funding options include bootstrapping, angel investors, venture capital, crowdfunding, bank loans, grants, and strategic partnerships.

Question 2: How should entrepreneurs determine the appropriate funding source for their business?

Answer: Entrepreneurs should consider their business stage, financial needs, growth plans, and the level of control they're willing to relinquish when selecting a funding source.

Question 3: What factors can impact an entrepreneur's ability to secure funding?

Answer: Factors such as the business's market potential, competitive advantage, financial projections, team expertise, and the entrepreneur's track record can influence funding decisions.

Question 4: How can entrepreneurs effectively pitch their business to potential investors?
Answer: A compelling pitch should clearly articulate the problem the business solves, the value proposition, market size, revenue model, competitive advantage, and the team's qualifications.
Question 5: What are the risks associated with different funding options, and how can entrepreneurs mitigate them?
Answer: Risks vary based on funding sources, such as equity dilution, repayment terms, or loss of control. Entrepreneurs should carefully review terms, seek legal counsel, and understand the implications.
"The best time to plant a tree was 20 years ago. The second best time is now." - Chinese Proverb
"Capital isn't scarce; vision is." - Sam Walton

Establishing a Solid Presence

Crafting a Memorable Brand Identity

In the dynamic landscape of entrepreneurship, the journey to success is often defined by the strength of a brand's identity. Just as a person's character shapes their reputation, a startup's brand identity influences how it's perceived by the world. This chapter delves into the art of crafting a memorable brand identity and explores the strategies that entrepreneurs can employ to establish a solid and enduring presence in the market.

A brand identity is more than just a logo; it's the essence of what a startup represents. This chapter underscores the pivotal role of branding in shaping perceptions, fostering connections, and differentiating a venture from its competitors. It highlights the symbiotic relationship between brand identity and business success, emphasizing that a cohesive and compelling brand identity is the cornerstone of a startup's growth.

The process of crafting a brand identity involves a blend of creativity and strategy. Entrepreneurs must delve into their startup's values, mission, and unique selling points to define the brand's personality. This chapter explores strategies for translating these foundational elements into visual design, messaging, and a cohesive brand voice that resonates with the target audience.

Moreover, the narrative delves into the significance of consistency in brand communication. Establishing a solid presence requires ensuring that every touchpoint—be it a social media post, website design, or customer service interaction—reflects the brand's identity cohesively. This chapter provides insights into maintaining a consistent brand experience that builds trust and recognition. Furthermore, the chapter addresses the role of authenticity in brand identity. In a world where transparency is valued, entrepreneurs are encouraged to build an authentic brand that aligns with their startup's values and resonates with customers on a genuine level. Authenticity not only fosters customer loyalty but also establishes a reputation that stands the test of time.

In conclusion, the journey to a strong market presence begins with the crafting of a brand identity that embodies a startup's essence and values. Through thoughtful design, consistent communication, and an authentic approach, entrepreneurs pave the way for a brand that captures hearts and leaves an indelible mark on the world.

Question 1: Why is a strong brand identity important for a business?
Answer: A strong brand identity differentiates a business, builds trust with customers, fosters recognition, and conveys the business's values and personality.

Question 2: What components make up a brand identity?
Answer: A brand identity includes a logo, color palette, typography, imagery style, tone of voice, and a consistent visual and emotional experience across all touchpoints.

Question 3: How can entrepreneurs align their brand identity with their target audience's preferences?
Answer: Conduct market research to understand audience preferences, values, and behaviors, then tailor the brand identity to resonate with those insights.

Question 4: How does a brand identity contribute to customer loyalty?
Answer: A consistent and appealing brand identity creates a strong impression, making customers more likely to remember, trust, and remain loyal to the business.

Question 5: Can a brand identity evolve over time, or should it remain consistent?
Answer: A brand identity can evolve to reflect growth, changing market trends, or shifts in the business's focus, but changes should be carefully managed to avoid confusing customers.

"Your brand is what people say about you when you're not in the room." - Jeff Bezos

"A brand is a voice and a product is a souvenir." - Lisa Gansky
"Your work is going to fill a large part of your life, and the only way to be truly satisfied is to do what you believe is great work." - Steve Jobs

Part III
Navigating Challenges
Overcoming Obstacles
Navigating Challenges
Overcoming Early Obstacles

In the dynamic and exhilarating landscape of entrepreneurship, the journey to success is not a straight path but a series of trials and triumphs. The early stages of a startup's existence are often characterized by a multitude of obstacles, each presenting an opportunity for growth and learning. This chapter explores the concept of navigating challenges and sheds light on strategies to overcome the myriad obstacles that entrepreneurs encounter in their pursuit of building a thriving business.

A Landscape of Trials: Understanding the Entrepreneurial Journey
The entrepreneurial journey is akin to embarking on an uncharted adventure. As entrepreneurs set forth to realize their vision, they encounter a variety of challenges that test their mettle, creativity, and determination. These challenges, though daunting, serve as transformative milestones that shape not only the business but also the individuals behind it.

A Tapestry of Obstacles: Common Challenges in the Early Stages
The early obstacles faced by startups are as diverse as they are formidable. From market validation and securing funding to managing cash flow, standing out in a competitive market, and nurturing a cohesive team, entrepreneurs are confronted with a myriad of trials that demand their strategic acumen and adaptability.

Market Validation: Navigating the Uncertainty
In the quest to bring an idea to market, one of the initial challenges is validating its demand. Entrepreneurs grapple with questions of

whether their product or service resonates with the intended audience. This challenge necessitates thorough market research, engagement with potential customers, and the creation of prototypes or pilot programs to gauge interest and viability.

Financial Frontiers: Securing Necessary Funding

Securing funding is a critical hurdle that many startups face. The challenge lies in convincing investors, be they angel investors, venture capitalists, or even personal savings, to believe in the potential of the idea. Crafting a compelling business plan, demonstrating a clear revenue model, and outlining the path to profitability become integral strategies in overcoming this obstacle.

Navigating the Ebb and Flow: Cash Flow Management

Startups often experience fluctuations in cash flow, which can impact their operations and growth. Entrepreneurs need to be adept at managing finances, forecasting future needs, and adopting measures to ensure the sustainability of the business during lean periods.

Standing Out Amidst the Crowd: Tackling Competition

In a competitive market, differentiation is key. The challenge is to carve a niche and establish a unique value proposition that sets the startup apart. Entrepreneurs must devise innovative strategies that resonate with their target audience and convey a distinctive brand identity.

Pivoting in Pursuit of Success: Adaptability in Strategy

Entrepreneurs might encounter a need to pivot their strategies as they learn from early experiences. This demands the ability to acknowledge the need for change and swiftly adapt to evolving market dynamics, customer feedback, and emerging trends.

The Dynamics of Team: Building Cohesion and Commitment

Nurturing a cohesive and committed team is paramount for startup success. The challenge lies in assembling individuals with diverse skills, aligning them with the startup's vision, and fostering a collaborative environment that thrives on open communication and mutual support.

Regulatory Realities: Ensuring Compliance and Legitimacy

Entrepreneurs must navigate the intricate landscape of regulations and legalities. The challenge is to ensure that the startup operates within the legal framework, acquires necessary licenses, and adheres to industry-specific standards.

Scaling Sustainably: Growth without Compromise

As startups experience growth, scalability becomes a challenge. Entrepreneurs must strategize how to expand operations, serve an increasing customer base, and maintain the quality that drove their initial success.

Understanding the Terrain: Identifying Common Challenges

The entrepreneurial journey is a dynamic terrain peppered with hurdles. Common challenges include market validation, securing funding, managing cash flow, competition, pivoting strategies, team dynamics, regulatory compliance, scaling, marketing effectiveness, and maintaining motivation.

Question 1: What are some common early obstacles that entrepreneurs may face?

Answer: Early obstacles can include limited resources, market entry barriers, regulatory challenges, competition, and the need to establish credibility in a new market.

Question 2: How can entrepreneurs effectively manage and navigate these challenges?

Answer: Entrepreneurs can manage challenges by conducting thorough research, seeking expert advice, remaining adaptable, focusing on solutions rather than problems, and leveraging networking opportunities.

Question 3: Can early obstacles provide valuable learning experiences for entrepreneurs?

Answer: Yes, overcoming challenges can lead to invaluable lessons that contribute to an entrepreneur's growth, problem-solving abilities, and overall business acumen.

Question 4: How important is resilience when facing early obstacles in entrepreneurship?

Answer: Resilience is crucial as it allows entrepreneurs to bounce back from setbacks, maintain focus on their goals, and stay motivated despite challenges.

Question 5: Can overcoming early obstacles lead to unexpected opportunities and advantages?

Answer: Yes, successfully navigating early obstacles can position entrepreneurs as industry experts, build a foundation of trust with customers, and uncover new pathways for growth.

"Challenges are what make life interesting, and overcoming them is what makes life meaningful." - Joshua J. Marine

Embracing Failure
Learning and Adapting from Setbacks

In the realm of entrepreneurship, failure is not a roadblock; it's a stepping stone. The journey to success is rarely linear, and setbacks are an inherent part of the landscape. This chapter delves into the concept of embracing failure as a catalyst for growth, learning, and adaptation—a philosophy that transforms stumbling blocks into valuable lessons.

The Crucible of Growth: Reframing Failure

Failure is not a mark of defeat; it's a crucible in which entrepreneurs forge resilience and wisdom. By reframing failure as a temporary setback rather than a definitive end, entrepreneurs open themselves up to the profound learning opportunities that it offers.

Learning from Missteps: Extracting Valuable Lessons

Every failure carries within it a treasure trove of insights. Analyzing the reasons behind the setback, identifying what went wrong, and understanding the contributing factors pave the way for improved strategies and more informed decisions in the future.

Adaptation as the Path Forward: Pivoting with Purpose

Failure often necessitates adaptation. Entrepreneurs who embrace failure recognize the need for strategic pivots. The ability to adjust strategies, refine approaches, and pivot when necessary is a hallmark of resilience and an integral component of entrepreneurial success.

Fostering a Growth Mindset: Cultivating Adaptability

Embracing failure is a testament to a growth mindset—a mental framework that sees challenges as opportunities rather than obstacles. Entrepreneurs with a growth mindset view setbacks as platforms for personal and professional development, fostering a mindset that thrives in the face of adversity.

Bouncing Back Stronger: From Setbacks to Success

The true measure of an entrepreneur's mettle lies not in avoiding failure, but in how they rise from it. By acknowledging setbacks, adapting strategies, and incorporating lessons learned, entrepreneurs can use the very failures that might have derailed them as catalysts to propel them toward future successes.

Question 1: Why is it important for entrepreneurs to view failure as a learning opportunity?

Answer: Viewing failure as a learning experience allows entrepreneurs to identify mistakes, adapt strategies, and make informed decisions that ultimately lead to greater success.

Question 2: How can entrepreneurs strike a balance between learning from failure and avoiding repeated mistakes?

Answer: Reflecting on failures, seeking feedback, and implementing changes based on lessons learned can help entrepreneurs avoid repeating the same mistakes.

Question 3: Can sharing failure stories with others benefit entrepreneurs?

Answer: Yes, sharing failure stories promotes transparency, helps remove the stigma associated with failure, and provides a platform for learning and growth.

Question 4: What role does emotional resilience play in embracing failure?

Answer: Emotional resilience helps entrepreneurs cope with the emotional impact of failure, maintain a positive attitude, and remain motivated to move forward.

Question 5: How can entrepreneurs build a supportive network to navigate failure effectively?

Answer: Building a network of mentors, peers, and advisors provides entrepreneurs with a supportive community that can offer guidance and encouragement during challenging times.

"Failure is the condiment that gives success its flavor." - Truman Capote

Growing Pains
Scaling Your Business Smartly

In the intricate tapestry of entrepreneurship, setbacks are not dead ends but rather crossroads that offer a choice—succumb to defeat or use adversity as a catalyst for growth. This chapter delves into the transformative power of overcoming setbacks, exploring how challenges can be harnessed as opportunities to adapt, innovate, and evolve.

The Landscape of Resilience: Shifting the Perspective

Setbacks are not indicators of inadequacy; they are stepping stones to resilience. Entrepreneurs who view setbacks as temporary setbacks rather than insurmountable obstacles open themselves up to a mindset that fosters adaptability and ongoing progress.

Harvesting Insights from Adversity: Lessons in Failure

Each setback contains a wealth of knowledge waiting to be unearthed. By closely examining the factors that contributed to the setback, entrepreneurs can glean valuable insights that inform future decisions, strategies, and approaches.

Adapting and Evolving: Navigating Change with Confidence
Setbacks often necessitate change, and embracing such change is a hallmark of resilience. Entrepreneurs who understand the importance of pivoting strategies and adapting to new circumstances transform challenges into opportunities for growth and development.

Cultivating a Growth Mindset: Thriving Amidst Challenges
Embracing setbacks requires a growth mindset—one that recognizes challenges as vehicles for growth and sees effort and resilience as the path to mastery. Entrepreneurs who foster a growth mindset are better equipped to persevere, innovate, and overcome even the most formidable obstacles.

From Setbacks to Success Stories: Rising Stronger
The journey of entrepreneurship is a testament to the art of overcoming setbacks. Entrepreneurs who transform challenges into stepping stones understand that the path to success is not paved in certainty but in the resilience to bounce back, recalibrate, and channel adversity into an unwavering drive toward future achievements.

"Success is not final, failure is not fatal: It is the courage to continue that counts." - Winston Churchill

Market Dynamics
Adapting to Changing Consumer Trends

In the dynamic realm of entrepreneurship, success hinges on a profound understanding of market dynamics—shifting currents that are influenced by ever-evolving consumer trends. This chapter delves into the crucial significance of staying attuned to changing consumer behaviors and explores strategies for adapting to these shifts to ensure continued relevance and growth.

The Fluid Landscape: Unraveling Market Dynamics
Market dynamics represent the intricate interplay between supply, demand, competition, and consumer preferences. To navigate this landscape successfully, entrepreneurs must grasp the nuances of these forces and their impact on their business trajectory.

Consumer Trends as the North Star: Guiding Business Evolution
Consumer trends serve as the compass that guides businesses toward prosperous shores. This chapter underscores the pivotal role of consumer

preferences, behaviors, and demands in shaping product development, marketing strategies, and overall business direction.

Adaptation in Action: Responding to Changing Tides

Entrepreneurs must be agile and adaptive to respond effectively to shifting consumer trends. This chapter delves into strategies for recognizing emerging trends, analyzing their implications, and pivoting strategies to align with evolving customer expectations.

Customer-Centric Approach: Personalizing Experiences

A key strategy for staying ahead in market dynamics is to adopt a customer-centric approach. Entrepreneurs who place their customers at the heart of their business decisions are better poised to anticipate and cater to changing needs, fostering loyalty and driving growth.

Innovation as a Response: Pioneering Change

In a landscape defined by rapid change, innovation becomes a potent response to evolving consumer trends. Entrepreneurs who continuously seek novel solutions, refine their offerings, and introduce fresh perspectives can capture the market's attention and secure a competitive advantage.

Strategic Partnerships: Amplifying Adaptation

Entrepreneurs can bolster their adaptability by forming strategic partnerships with industry players and experts. Collaborative ventures enable businesses to leverage shared insights, pool resources, and gain a deeper understanding of market dynamics.

The Kaleidoscope of Change: Thriving Amidst Fluidity

Market dynamics are akin to a kaleidoscope, each turn revealing new patterns and possibilities. Entrepreneurs who embrace this fluidity, welcome change, and view consumer trends as opportunities rather than challenges position themselves to flourish in an ever-evolving marketplace.

Question 1: Why is it important for entrepreneurs to stay attuned to changing consumer trends?

Answer: Adapting to changing trends allows entrepreneurs to remain relevant, anticipate customer needs, and position their offerings ahead of competitors.

Question 2: How can entrepreneurs gather insights about shifting consumer preferences?

Answer: Conducting market research, monitoring social media discussions, analyzing customer feedback, and studying industry reports can provide insights into changing consumer trends.

Question 3: Can adapting to consumer trends involve changes beyond product offerings?

Answer: Yes, adapting to trends can involve changes in marketing strategies, customer engagement methods, and even business models to align with evolving consumer behaviors.

Question 4: What challenges might entrepreneurs face when trying to adapt to changing trends?

Answer: Challenges may include the need for rapid adjustments, resource allocation, and the risk of misinterpreting trends or overhauling established strategies too quickly.

Question 5: How can entrepreneurs balance responding to current trends with maintaining a consistent brand identity?

Answer: Entrepreneurs can strike a balance by aligning trend adaptations with their brand's core values and long-term vision, ensuring that changes enhance rather than dilute the brand identity.

"The best way to predict the future is to create it." - Peter Drucker

"I have not failed. I've just found 10,000 ways that won't work." - Thomas A. Edison

---

Important questions

Market Validation: Ensuring Demand

Q: How do I ensure there's a demand for my product/service?

A: Conduct thorough market research, gather feedback from potential customers, and validate your concept through prototypes or minimum viable products.

Securing Funding: Overcoming Financial Hurdles

Q: What if I can't secure funding for my startup?

A: Explore alternative funding sources, such as bootstrapping, crowdfunding, or seeking angel investors. Ensure your business plan is comprehensive and convincing.

Cash Flow Management: Navigating Financial Fluctuations

Q: How do I manage cash flow challenges in the early stages?

A: Create a detailed financial plan, monitor expenses rigorously, maintain a cushion for unexpected costs, and negotiate favorable terms with suppliers.

Competition: Standing Out in the Crowd

Q: How do I differentiate my startup in a competitive market?

A: Define a unique value proposition, focus on exceptional customer service, innovate continuously, and create a compelling brand identity.

Pivoting Strategies: Adapting to Change

Q: What if my initial strategies aren't working?
A: Be open to pivoting. Analyze feedback, data, and market trends, and adjust your strategies accordingly.

Team Dynamics: Nurturing Cohesion
Q: How do I address conflicts within my team?
A: Foster open communication, establish clear roles and expectations, promote collaboration, and address conflicts promptly.

Regulatory Compliance: Navigating Legalities
Q: How do I ensure my startup adheres to legal requirements?
A: Research regulations in your industry and location, consult legal experts, and obtain necessary licenses and permits.

Scaling: Growing Sustainably
Q: How do I scale without compromising quality?
A: Plan for scalability from the start, optimize processes, invest in technology, and hire strategically.

Marketing Effectiveness: Reaching the Right Audience
Q: How do I ensure my marketing efforts are effective?
A: Define your target audience, tailor your marketing strategies to their preferences, track and analyze results, and be ready to iterate.

Maintaining Motivation: Overcoming Setbacks
Q: How do I stay motivated in the face of challenges?
A: Set realistic goals, celebrate small victories, seek mentorship, maintain a healthy work-life balance, and remind yourself of your initial passion and vision.

In conclusion, the early stages of entrepreneurship are a labyrinth of challenges, each offering an opportunity for growth and learning. By approaching obstacles with a strategic mindset, seeking guidance when needed, and embracing the inevitability of setbacks, entrepreneurs can navigate these challenges and emerge stronger, more resilient, and better equipped to lead their startups to success. Remember, the journey to triumph is often paved with the stones of adversity.

Part IV
Igniting Growth - Expanding Horizons

Igniting Growth
Expanding Your Horizons

In the thrilling journey of entrepreneurship, the pursuit of growth is a constant beacon guiding ventures toward new horizons of success. This chapter explores the art of igniting growth and delves into strategies that empower entrepreneurs to expand their ventures, seize opportunities, and reach remarkable heights.

Understanding Growth: A Journey of Evolution

Growth is the heartbeat of entrepreneurship, propelling startups from inception to establishment and beyond. It's a journey that involves embracing change, seizing opportunities, and daring to venture into uncharted territories.

What Does Growth Entail?

Growth encompasses a broad spectrum, from increasing revenue and market share to expanding into new markets, developing new products, and enhancing brand recognition. It's a multifaceted progression that demands a holistic approach.

Navigating Expansion: Scaling Strategically

The path to growth often involves scaling—a strategic process that requires careful planning, resource allocation, and an understanding of market dynamics. Entrepreneurs must identify the right timing and methodologies to scale without compromising quality.

When Is the Right Time to Expand?

The right time to expand varies based on factors such as market readiness, financial stability, and operational capacity. Entrepreneurs should assess whether their current position and resources align with the potential for successful expansion.

Market Research: Identifying New Avenues

Growth begins with thorough market research. Entrepreneurs must identify untapped markets, emerging trends, and customer needs to tailor their expansion strategy and position themselves for success.

Diversification: Mitigating Risk Through Variety

Diversification is a strategy that involves expanding into different markets, products, or services. It mitigates risk by reducing reliance on a single revenue stream and allows entrepreneurs to leverage their strengths across diverse areas.

What Risks Does Expansion Entail?

Expansion introduces risks such as increased competition, operational challenges, and resource constraints. Entrepreneurs must conduct comprehensive risk assessments and develop contingency plans to navigate potential pitfalls.

Cultivating Innovation: Fueling Sustained Growth

Innovation is the lifeblood of sustained growth. Entrepreneurs should foster a culture of creativity, encourage the exploration of new ideas, and invest in research and development to keep their offerings relevant and compelling.

How Can Technology Facilitate Growth?

Technology plays a pivotal role in modern business growth. It streamlines operations, enhances customer experiences, and opens new avenues for reaching wider audiences, making technology adoption a strategic imperative.

Maintaining Core Values: Staying True While Expanding

As startups grow, it's crucial to maintain their core values and the essence that made them unique. Entrepreneurs should ensure that expansion efforts align with their initial vision, fostering authenticity and customer trust.

"The secret to change is to focus all your energy not on fighting the old but on building the new." - Socrates

"The biggest risk is not taking any risk. In a world that is changing quickly, the only strategy that is guaranteed to fail is not taking risks." - Mark Zuckerberg

Question 1: How do I know if my startup is ready for expansion?

Answer: Look for signs such as consistent demand, a strong customer base, sustainable revenue, and the ability to scale operations efficiently.

Question 2: What are the potential benefits of diversifying my product or service offerings?

Answer: Diversification can reduce risk by not relying on a single revenue stream, open new markets, and attract a broader customer base.

Question 3: What strategies can I use to ensure that expanding doesn't compromise the quality of my products or services?
Answer: Invest in systems, processes, and training to maintain consistent quality standards as you scale.
Question 4: How can I identify new markets or customer segments for expansion?
Answer: Conduct thorough market research to identify untapped opportunities, analyze demographics, and assess customer needs in new markets.
Question 5: What role does branding play in the expansion process?
Answer: Branding is crucial for consistency and recognition. Ensure your brand message and identity resonate across new markets.
Question 6: How do I secure the necessary resources, such as funding and talent, to support expansion?
Answer: Develop a comprehensive business plan that outlines your growth strategy and financial needs. Consider seeking external funding or partnerships.
Question 7: What challenges should I anticipate when expanding internationally or into new geographic regions?
Answer: Challenges may include cultural differences, regulatory hurdles, and adapting to local market preferences.
Question 8: How can I maintain effective communication and cohesion within my team during expansion?
Answer: Establish clear communication channels, delegate responsibilities, and provide ongoing training to ensure everyone is aligned with the expansion goals.
Question 9: How can I effectively manage increased demand while scaling my operations?
Answer: Invest in technology to streamline processes, consider outsourcing non-core functions, and hire strategically to meet increased demand.
Question 10: What metrics and indicators should I monitor to track the success of my expansion efforts?
Answer: Key performance indicators (KPIs) could include revenue growth, customer acquisition rate, customer retention, and market share in new regions.

Innovating for Success
Rethinking Products and Services

In the dynamic landscape of entrepreneurship, innovation is not a luxury; it's a necessity. The pursuit of success demands constant adaptation and the ability to think beyond the conventional. This chapter delves into the art of innovating for success—reimagining products and services to meet evolving customer needs, seize untapped opportunities, and stay ahead in a competitive market.

The Imperative of Innovation: Pioneering Change

Innovation is the engine that propels businesses forward. Entrepreneurs who embrace innovation recognize that stagnation is a greater risk than change. The landscape is ever-evolving, and the ability to innovate is a strategic advantage that can ensure long-term relevance and prosperity.

Rethinking Customer Needs: The Catalyst for Innovation

Successful innovation is rooted in an intimate understanding of customer needs. Entrepreneurs must engage in empathetic exploration—listening to customer feedback, analyzing market trends, and staying attuned to shifting preferences—to identify gaps that innovative solutions can fill.

From Incremental to Disruptive: Navigating Innovation Spectrum

Innovation takes many forms, from incremental improvements to radical disruption. Entrepreneurs can explore incremental innovation by refining existing products or services, or they can embark on disruptive innovation by revolutionizing entire industries with game-changing solutions.

Prototyping and Experimentation: Pioneering New Horizons

Innovation is not a one-shot endeavor; it's a journey of experimentation and iteration. Entrepreneurs should embrace prototyping, testing, and adapting their ideas based on real-world feedback. This iterative process minimizes risk and enhances the chances of success.

Revolutionizing Business Models: Expanding Boundaries

Innovation isn't limited to products; it extends to business models. Entrepreneurs can reimagine how they deliver value to customers, exploring subscription models, platform ecosystems, and sharing economy concepts to open new avenues for growth.

Creating a Culture of Innovation: Nurturing Creativity

Fostering a culture of innovation is a strategic imperative. Entrepreneurs should encourage a mindset where creativity is celebrated, risk-taking is supported, and employees are empowered to contribute ideas. A culture that values innovation can lead to a steady stream of breakthroughs.

Innovation thrives in agile environments. Entrepreneurs who build flexible structures can quickly pivot their strategies based on market feedback and changing trends. This adaptability is a cornerstone of successful innovation.

In conclusion, the journey to success in entrepreneurship is paved with innovation. Entrepreneurs who understand the significance of rethinking products, services, and business models can not only respond to customer needs but anticipate them. By fostering a culture of creativity, staying attuned to market dynamics, and embracing experimentation, entrepreneurs can position themselves to lead the charge of innovation and chart a course toward lasting success.

Question 1: Why is innovation important for the long-term success of a business?

Answer: Innovation keeps a business competitive by introducing new ideas, products, and services that meet evolving customer needs and capitalize on emerging trends.

Question 2: How can entrepreneurs foster a culture of innovation within their company?

Answer: Entrepreneurs can encourage innovation by fostering open communication, valuing diverse perspectives, allocating time for brainstorming, and rewarding creative thinking.

Question 3: Can innovation involve incremental improvements as well as disruptive changes?

Answer: Yes, innovation can encompass both small improvements and groundbreaking changes. Incremental innovations refine existing products, while disruptive innovations introduce entirely new solutions.

Question 4: How can entrepreneurs generate innovative ideas for their products or services?

Answer: Idea generation can come from customer feedback, market research, observing industry trends, engaging in cross-disciplinary thinking, and encouraging experimentation.

Question 5: What are some challenges entrepreneurs might face when implementing innovative changes?

Answer: Challenges may include resistance to change, resource constraints, the risk of failure, and ensuring that changes align with the brand's core values and customer expectations.

"Innovation distinguishes between a leader and a follower." - Steve Jobs

Building a Loyal Following
Leveraging Customer Relationship Management

In the dynamic world of entrepreneurship, building a loyal customer following is the cornerstone of sustainable success. Central to this endeavor is the art of Customer Relationship Management (CRM), a strategic approach that empowers businesses to cultivate strong connections, understand customer needs, and foster enduring brand loyalty. This chapter delves into the realm of leveraging CRM to build a loyal following, exploring strategies that allow entrepreneurs to transform casual customers into enthusiastic advocates.

The Power of Relationships: Nurturing Customer Connections

At the heart of successful entrepreneurship lies the ability to forge meaningful relationships with customers. CRM is the tool that facilitates this connection by enabling businesses to understand their customers, personalize interactions, and deliver tailored value propositions.

Understanding Customer Needs: A Pillar of CRM

CRM begins with comprehending customer needs on a granular level. By collecting data and insights, entrepreneurs can anticipate preferences, identify pain points, and tailor their offerings to provide maximum value.

Personalization for Engagement: Elevating Customer Experiences

Customers seek personalized experiences that resonate with their individual preferences. CRM empowers entrepreneurs to deliver relevant content, product recommendations, and promotions, creating engagement that deepens brand affinity.

Data-Driven Insights: Informing Strategic Decisions

CRM generates a treasure trove of data, offering insights into purchasing behaviors, preferences, and trends. Entrepreneurs can harness this data to refine marketing strategies, optimize product development, and make informed business decisions.

Enhancing Customer Support. A CRM Imperative

Exceptional customer support is a hallmark of CRM. Businesses can use CRM systems to track customer interactions, respond promptly to inquiries, and resolve issues, fostering trust and loyalty.

Building Loyalty Programs: Rewarding Devotion

CRM allows entrepreneurs to design loyalty programs that reward customers for their repeat business. These programs incentivize engagement, encourage referrals, and solidify relationships.

Measuring ROI: Quantifying CRM Impact

A critical aspect of CRM implementation is measuring its impact. Entrepreneurs can analyze key metrics such as customer retention rates, repeat purchases, and referral rates to gauge the effectiveness of their CRM strategies.

Omnichannel Engagement: Seamless Interactions

In the digital age, customers engage with businesses across multiple channels. CRM enables entrepreneurs to maintain a cohesive presence across platforms, delivering consistent experiences that reinforce brand loyalty.

Ethical Data Usage: Building Trust Through Transparency

As data becomes integral to CRM, entrepreneurs must prioritize ethical data usage. Transparency in data collection and usage builds trust, fostering an environment where customers willingly share insights.

In conclusion, Customer Relationship Management is not merely a software system—it's a philosophy that places customers at the heart of business strategies. Entrepreneurs who harness the power of CRM to deeply understand their customers, tailor experiences, and foster meaningful connections are poised to create a loyal following that not only supports their success but actively champions their brand. In the age of empowered consumers, CRM is the compass that guides businesses toward enduring customer loyalty.

Question 1: Why is building customer loyalty essential for sustainable business growth?

Answer: Loyal customers contribute to repeat business, positive word-of-mouth, and lower customer acquisition costs, resulting in increased profitability and long-term success.

Question 2: How can entrepreneurs cultivate strong relationships with their customers?

Answer: Entrepreneurs can engage with customers through personalized communication, offering exceptional customer service, seeking feedback, and consistently delivering value.

Question 3: What is the role of technology in customer relationship management?

Answer: Technology tools, such as customer relationship management (CRM) software, enable entrepreneurs to track customer interactions, personalize communication, and manage customer data efficiently.

Question 4: Can customer loyalty extend beyond the product or service itself?

Answer: Yes, customer loyalty can be enhanced by creating a positive brand experience, building a sense of community, and demonstrating shared values with customers.

Question 5: How can entrepreneurs measure the success of their customer relationship management efforts?

Answer: Metrics such as customer retention rates, customer satisfaction scores, repeat purchase frequency, and net promoter scores provide insights into the effectiveness of CRM strategies.

"Your most unhappy customers are your greatest source of learning." - Bill Gates

Expanding to New Markets
Seizing Global Opportunities

In the dynamic realm of entrepreneurship, the allure of global markets beckons as a realm of untapped potential. Expanding to new markets is a strategic leap that promises growth, diversity, and the chance to connect with a broader audience. This chapter delves into the exciting journey of seizing global opportunities, exploring strategies that empower entrepreneurs to navigate cultural nuances, regulatory landscapes, and consumer behaviors to achieve successful international expansion.

Unveiling New Horizons: The Promise of Global Expansion
Expanding to new markets is an adventure that invites entrepreneurs to stretch beyond familiar boundaries. It's a strategic move that demands careful consideration, robust planning, and a deep understanding of the unique dynamics of each target market.

Mapping Market Landscapes: The Core of International Strategy
Successful global expansion begins with meticulous market research. Entrepreneurs must delve into cultural differences, economic trends, competitive landscapes, and consumer behaviors to tailor their strategies to suit the nuances of each market.

Navigating Cultural Nuances: Building Bridges Across Borders
Cultural sensitivity is a cornerstone of international expansion. Entrepreneurs must understand local customs, language, values, and preferences to ensure that their offerings resonate authentically with new audiences.

Regulatory Realities: Adapting to Legal and Regulatory Frameworks
Each market comes with its own set of regulations and compliance requirements. Entrepreneurs must navigate these complexities, obtain necessary licenses, and adhere to local laws to establish a legitimate and sustainable presence.

Customizing Offerings: Tailoring Products and Services for Global Audiences

A one-size-fits-all approach doesn't suffice in global markets. Entrepreneurs should customize their offerings to cater to local tastes, preferences, and needs, demonstrating a commitment to understanding and serving diverse customers.

Distribution and Logistics: Efficiently Reaching Global Audiences

An effective distribution and logistics strategy is essential for global success. Entrepreneurs must strategize how to efficiently transport products, manage supply chains, and ensure timely deliveries across borders.

Communication Across Borders: Crafting Global Brand Messaging

Consistent and culturally sensitive communication is paramount. Entrepreneurs should adapt their branding and marketing messages to resonate with local audiences while maintaining the essence of their brand identity.

Risk Management: Mitigating Challenges of International Expansion

Global expansion introduces a spectrum of risks, from currency fluctuations to geopolitical uncertainties. Entrepreneurs must develop comprehensive risk management strategies to safeguard their ventures.

Local Partnerships: Leveraging Expertise and Networks

Collaborating with local partners—whether distributors, suppliers, or industry experts—can provide invaluable insights and networks that enhance the chances of successful market entry.

Global expansion is a strategic pursuit that requires foresight, adaptability, and a deep respect for cultural diversity. Entrepreneurs who seize the opportunities presented by new markets while remaining attuned to the challenges can unlock a world of growth and success. With a blend of meticulous research, cultural sensitivity, and a willingness to adapt, international expansion becomes a transformative journey toward expanding horizons.

Question 1: What are the potential benefits of expanding a business to new markets?

Answer: Expanding to new markets can lead to increased revenue, diversification of risks, access to new customer segments, and opportunities for growth and innovation.

Question 2: How can entrepreneurs identify viable opportunities for global expansion?

Answer: Market research, identifying cultural fit, evaluating competition, considering regulatory factors, and analyzing economic conditions are essential for identifying potential markets.

Question 3: What challenges might entrepreneurs encounter when entering new markets?
Answer: Challenges may include cultural differences, regulatory hurdles, understanding local customer preferences, distribution logistics, and managing a geographically dispersed team.
Question 4: What strategies can entrepreneurs use to adapt their offerings to new markets?
Answer: Adapting offerings involves understanding local preferences, tailoring marketing messages, adjusting pricing strategies, and considering product localization.
Question 5: How can entrepreneurs manage the risks associated with global expansion?
Answer: Mitigating risks involves thorough market research, seeking local partnerships, consulting legal and regulatory experts, and developing contingency plans to navigate challenges.

"The world is a book, and those who do not travel read only one page." - Augustine of Hippo

"Think globally, act locally." - Patrick Geddes

" The biggest risk is not taking any risk. In a world that's changing quickly, the only strategy that is guaranteed to fail is not taking risks." - Mark Zuckerberg

Part V
Sustaining Excellence
Thriving in the Long Run
Sustaining Excellence
Thriving in the Long Run

In the dynamic landscape of entrepreneurship, the pursuit of excellence is not a fleeting endeavor but an enduring commitment. Sustaining excellence is the hallmark of a business that thrives in the long run—a journey that demands consistent innovation, unwavering dedication, and a relentless pursuit of continuous improvement. This chapter delves into the art of sustaining excellence, exploring strategies that empower entrepreneurs to navigate challenges, adapt to changing times, and cultivate a legacy of enduring success.

The Essence of Excellence: Beyond Immediate Triumph

Excellence is not confined to fleeting victories; it's a philosophy that permeates every facet of a business. It's the commitment to delivering unparalleled value, maintaining high standards, and persistently striving to surpass even one's own achievements.

Cultivating a Culture of Excellence: A Core Foundation

Sustaining excellence begins with fostering a culture that values innovation, accountability, and continuous learning. Entrepreneurs must create an environment where excellence is not an expectation but a natural outcome.

Innovation as a Compass: Pioneering Ongoing Improvement

Excellence thrives on innovation. Entrepreneurs should constantly challenge the status quo, embrace change, and be willing to reinvent products, services, and processes to keep their offerings relevant and cutting-edge.

Customer-Centric Approach: The Key to Longevity

Excellence is inexorably tied to customer satisfaction. Entrepreneurs who prioritize understanding customer needs, providing exceptional service, and continuously exceeding expectations are positioned for enduring success.

Adaptation to Change: Embracing Evolutionary Shifts

Sustaining excellence requires adaptability. Entrepreneurs must stay attuned to market trends, customer preferences, and technological advancements, and be prepared to pivot their strategies to align with evolving dynamics.

Empowering the Team: Nurturing Excellence in Individuals

Excellence is a collective endeavor that stems from the efforts of a skilled and motivated team. Entrepreneurs should invest in employee development, provide opportunities for growth, and foster an atmosphere of collaboration and innovation.

Ethical Leadership: The Bedrock of Long-Term Excellence

Leadership that embodies ethical principles is pivotal to sustained excellence. Entrepreneurs should prioritize transparency, integrity, and social responsibility, earning the trust and respect of both customers and employees.

Measuring Success: Metrics Beyond Profits

While financial success is a crucial aspect, entrepreneurs must also measure excellence through non-financial indicators such as customer satisfaction, employee engagement, and impact on the community.

Resilience in Adversity: Navigating Challenges

Sustaining excellence doesn't imply immunity from challenges; rather, it's about demonstrating resilience in the face of adversity. Entrepreneurs should view setbacks as opportunities to innovate, learn, and grow stronger.

Leaving a Legacy: The Impact of Sustained Excellence

Excellence isn't just a pursuit of the present—it's a gift to the future. Entrepreneurs who sustain excellence create legacies that inspire, uplift, and serve as blueprints for generations to come.

sustaining excellence is a journey of purpose and dedication. Entrepreneurs who view excellence as an ongoing quest, not an end destination, are equipped to thrive amidst changing tides. By fostering a culture of innovation, embracing adaptability, and prioritizing ethical leadership, businesses can not only achieve enduring success but also create a legacy that stands the test of time.

Question 1: How can entrepreneurs ensure their business maintains long-term success?

Answer: Entrepreneurs can sustain excellence by staying adaptable, embracing continuous learning, remaining customer-focused, nurturing their team, and consistently innovating.

Question 2: What role does strategic planning play in sustaining excellence?

Answer: Strategic planning helps entrepreneurs anticipate challenges, set clear goals, allocate resources effectively, and proactively respond to changes in the market.

Question 3: Can sustaining excellence involve reevaluating and adjusting the business model over time?

Answer: Yes, reevaluating the business model and adapting to changing market conditions is essential for ensuring the business remains relevant and competitive.

Question 4: How can entrepreneurs foster a culture of excellence within their organization?

Answer: Entrepreneurs can foster excellence by setting high standards, recognizing and rewarding outstanding performance, encouraging collaboration, and leading by example.

Question 5: What strategies can entrepreneurs use to remain motivated and passionate about their business journey over the long term?

Answer: Setting personal goals, practicing self-care, seeking inspiration from mentors and successful entrepreneurs, and regularly celebrating milestones can help maintain motivation.

"Excellence is never an accident. It is always the result of high intention, sincere effort, and intelligent execution." - Aristotle

"Perfection is not attainable, but if we chase perfection we can catch excellence." - Vince Lombardi

Staying Ahead of Competition

Monitoring and Adapting to Industry Trends

In the fast-paced world of entrepreneurship, the race for success is often marked by the pursuit of staying ahead of the competition. Thriving in a competitive landscape demands more than mere survival—it requires a proactive approach that involves keenly monitoring industry trends, adapting to emerging shifts, and continuously innovating to maintain a leading edge. This chapter explores the art of staying ahead of the competition by effectively monitoring trends and strategically adapting to them.

The Competitive Arena: Navigating a Dynamic Landscape

Competition is an inherent part of entrepreneurship. Entrepreneurs who rise above the rest recognize that maintaining a competitive advantage is an ongoing commitment that involves vigilance, agility, and a relentless drive to evolve.

Unveiling Industry Trends: The Path to Strategic Advantage

Staying ahead necessitates a deep understanding of industry trends. Entrepreneurs must actively scan the horizon for emerging technologies, changing consumer behaviors, and evolving market dynamics that can shape the trajectory of their business.

Embracing Data-Driven Insights: A Strategic Imperative

Effective trend monitoring relies on data-driven insights. Entrepreneurs can leverage data analytics and market research to uncover patterns, make informed decisions, and anticipate shifts before they impact their business.

Agile Adaptation: The Key to Survival

Adaptation is the linchpin of staying competitive. Entrepreneurs should be prepared to pivot their strategies, refine their offerings, and innovate rapidly in response to changing trends, customer preferences, and technological advancements.

Customer-Centric Focus: Aligning with Evolving Needs

Staying ahead involves a deep connection with customers. Entrepreneurs who listen attentively to customer feedback, anticipate their changing needs, and tailor their offerings accordingly position themselves for sustained relevance.

Innovative Mindset: Cultivating a Culture of Creativity

An innovative mindset is central to maintaining a competitive edge. Entrepreneurs should foster an environment where creativity is celebrated, risks are embraced, and employees are encouraged to contribute fresh ideas.

Strategic Partnerships: Amplifying Competitive Advantage

Collaborations with strategic partners can enhance competitiveness. Entrepreneurs can pool resources, leverage complementary expertise, and tap into new networks to collectively navigate industry trends.

In conclusion, the journey of staying ahead of the competition is a continuous pursuit that demands agility, foresight, and the willingness to challenge the status quo. By meticulously monitoring industry trends, adapting proactively, and fostering a culture of innovation, entrepreneurs can transcend the boundaries of competition and lead the charge in shaping the future of their industry.

Question 1: Why is it important for entrepreneurs to monitor industry trends and competitor activities?

Answer: Monitoring trends and competitors enables entrepreneurs to identify emerging opportunities, stay ahead of disruptions, and make informed strategic decisions.

Question 2: How can entrepreneurs effectively gather and analyze information about industry trends?

Answer: Entrepreneurs can stay informed through industry publications, market research reports, attending conferences, networking, and leveraging data analytics.

Question 3: Can staying ahead of competition involve collaborating with competitors?

Answer: Collaborations with competitors, such as partnerships or joint ventures, can lead to mutually beneficial outcomes, including sharing resources and accessing new markets.

Question 4: What is the balance between adapting to trends and maintaining the business's core identity?

Answer: Entrepreneurs should adapt to trends that align with their core values and long-term vision, ensuring that changes enhance rather than dilute their brand identity.

Question 5: How does staying ahead of competition contribute to the overall resilience of a business?

Answer: Staying informed and adaptable helps businesses proactively respond to challenges, capitalize on emerging opportunities, and maintain relevance in dynamic markets.

"Success is walking from failure to failure with no loss of enthusiasm." - Winston Churchill

Ethical Entrepreneurship
Building a Sustainable and Responsible Business

In the modern landscape of entrepreneurship, success is no longer solely measured by financial gains; it's also assessed by the impact a business has on society and the environment. Ethical entrepreneurship is a paradigm shift that embraces social responsibility and sustainability as integral components of business success. This chapter explores the profound concept of ethical entrepreneurship, delving into the strategies that empower entrepreneurs to build businesses that not only thrive economically but also contribute positively to the world.

The Evolution of Entrepreneurship: A Shift Towards Ethics

Ethical entrepreneurship represents a departure from traditional profit-centric models. Entrepreneurs who embrace this ethos recognize that a business's long-term viability is intertwined with its ethical practices, social contributions, and environmental stewardship.

Sustainability as a Foundation: Nurturing a Greener Tomorrow

Sustainability is at the core of ethical entrepreneurship. Entrepreneurs must consider the environmental impact of their operations, adopt eco-friendly practices, and make conscious choices that safeguard natural resources for future generations.

Social Impact: Beyond Profit to Purpose

Ethical entrepreneurship extends beyond the balance sheet to the lives it touches. Entrepreneurs should actively seek ways to positively impact society, whether by creating job opportunities, supporting local communities, or championing social causes.

Ethical Supply Chains: Upholding Human Dignity

Ethical entrepreneurship involves a commitment to ethical supply chains. Entrepreneurs should ensure that their products are sourced responsibly, free from exploitative practices, and that fair wages are paid to all involved.

Transparent Practices: Building Trust Through Honesty

Transparency is a cornerstone of ethical entrepreneurship. Entrepreneurs should maintain open communication, uphold ethical standards, and be forthright about their practices, fostering trust among customers, partners, and stakeholders.

Balancing Profit and Purpose: A Delicate Equilibrium

Ethical entrepreneurship involves striking a balance between financial success and social responsibility. Entrepreneurs must navigate this delicate equilibrium, ensuring that ethical practices do not compromise business viability.

Advocacy and Education: Influencing Wider Change

Ethical entrepreneurs have the power to drive systemic change. They can use their platforms to advocate for ethical business practices, raise awareness about pressing issues, and inspire others to adopt responsible entrepreneurship.

In conclusion, ethical entrepreneurship transcends the confines of profit maximization. Entrepreneurs who embrace this ethos recognize that their businesses wield the power to create positive change, uplift communities, and protect the planet. By integrating sustainability, social impact, and transparency into their business strategies, ethical entrepreneurs not only build sustainable and responsible businesses but also set a precedent for a more just and equitable world.

Question 1: What is the significance of ethical entrepreneurship in today's business landscape?

Answer: Ethical entrepreneurship promotes social responsibility, sustainable practices, and trust among customers, employees, and stakeholders.

Question 2: How can entrepreneurs ensure their business operations align with ethical values?

Answer: Entrepreneurs can implement ethical practices by prioritizing transparency, valuing diversity and inclusion, minimizing environmental impact, and treating employees and customers with respect.

Question 3: Can ethical entrepreneurship lead to business advantages beyond ethical considerations?

Answer: Yes, ethical businesses often enjoy enhanced brand reputation, customer loyalty, and employee morale, which can translate to long-term success and profitability.

Question 4: How can entrepreneurs address ethical dilemmas that may arise in their business journey?

Answer: Addressing ethical dilemmas involves seeking advice from mentors, ethical experts, and legal professionals, and making decisions that prioritize the well-being of stakeholders.

Question 5: What strategies can entrepreneurs employ to communicate their commitment to ethical entrepreneurship to their stakeholders?
Answer: Entrepreneurs can communicate through transparent reporting, incorporating ethical considerations into marketing and branding efforts, and actively engaging in community initiatives.

"The best way to predict the future is to create it." - Peter Drucker

"It's hard to beat a person who never gives up." - Babe Ruth

Question 1: How can I integrate sustainability practices into my business operations and supply chains?
Answer: You can begin by conducting an assessment of your current practices to identify areas for improvement. Implement eco-friendly processes, reduce waste, and source materials responsibly. Consider partnerships with suppliers that share your commitment to sustainability.

Question 2: What steps can I take to ensure that my products and services are produced ethically and do not harm the environment?
Answer: Prioritize ethical sourcing by verifying suppliers' labor practices and environmental standards. Embrace eco-friendly production methods and materials. Conduct lifecycle assessments to minimize environmental impact.

Question 3: How do I balance the financial success of my business with the ethical and social impact it has on society?
Answer: Striking this balance requires strategic planning. Incorporate social responsibility into your business strategy. Consider long-term benefits such as enhanced brand reputation and customer loyalty that ethical practices can bring.

Question 4: What strategies can I implement to actively contribute to the well-being of the communities in which I operate?
Answer: Engage with local communities through initiatives such as job creation, skill development, and support for community projects. Listen to community needs and involve stakeholders in decision-making processes.

Question 5: How can I communicate my commitment to ethical practices and sustainability to customers and stakeholders?
Answer: Transparent communication is key. Highlight your ethical initiatives on your website and through social media. Use packaging and marketing materials to convey your commitment to sustainability and responsible business practices.

Question 6: What partnerships or collaborations can I pursue to amplify my impact and drive positive change in my industry?
Answer: Collaborate with NGOs, industry associations, and like-minded businesses to pool resources and expertise. Participate in industry events focused on sustainability to learn from others and share best practices.

Question 7: What methods can I use to measure the social and environmental impact of my business efforts?

Answer: Implement key performance indicators (KPIs) related to sustainability and social impact. Measure metrics such as carbon footprint reduction, employee satisfaction, and community engagement to track progress.

Question 8: How do I navigate potential challenges or trade-offs between profitability and ethical practices?

Answer: Recognize that ethical practices can lead to long-term benefits, including customer loyalty and positive brand perception. Evaluate the cost-benefit analysis of ethical choices and consider the potential positive impact on your business's reputation.

Question 9: What role can innovation play in creating sustainable solutions and driving positive change in my industry?

Answer: Innovation can drive sustainability. Seek creative ways to reduce waste, enhance efficiency, and create products with a lower environmental footprint. Innovate for circular business models that promote reuse and recycling.

Question 10: How can I engage and educate my employees, customers, and partners about the importance of ethical entrepreneurship and sustainability?

Answer: Internal and external education is crucial. Train employees on ethical practices and sustainability initiatives. Educate customers through marketing materials, blog posts, and interactive events. Engage partners in conversations about shared values and goals.

Leading with Purpose

Becoming an Inspirational Business Leader

In the realm of entrepreneurship, leadership transcends conventional management; it's a calling to inspire, empower, and shape the trajectory of both businesses and individuals. Leading with purpose is a transformative approach that goes beyond profit-driven objectives. It centers on infusing every action with a deeper meaning, fostering a positive impact on employees, customers, and society at large. This chapter delves into the profound concept of leading with purpose—how it transcends transactional leadership, the qualities that define an inspirational business leader, and the path to becoming a catalyst for positive change.

Purpose as the North Star: Redefining Leadership

Leadership with purpose is a paradigm shift that acknowledges the profound impact a business leader can have. It's an invitation to operate beyond short-term gains, emphasizing the long-term vision, values, and societal contribution of an organization.

Empowering Others: The Essence of Inspirational Leadership

At the heart of leading with purpose is the empowerment of others. Inspirational business leaders understand that their role is not to command but to enable their teams, fostering an environment where individuals thrive, take ownership, and contribute their best.

Visionary Clarity: Charting a Path Toward Transformation

Inspirational leaders possess a crystal-clear vision that guides their actions. They articulate a compelling narrative that ignites passion, unites teams, and mobilizes efforts toward a shared purpose.

Values as Compass: Upholding Integrity and Ethics

Ethical conduct and values-driven decisions are hallmarks of inspirational leadership. Leaders who lead with purpose prioritize integrity, honesty, and ethical decision-making, setting a high standard for both their teams and the industry.

Cultivating Emotional Intelligence: Connecting on a Human Level

Inspirational leaders understand the significance of emotional intelligence. They forge authentic connections, listen attentively, and demonstrate empathy, creating a sense of belonging and trust among their teams.

Leading by Example: Role Modeling Excellence

The most effective form of leadership is that which leads by example. Inspirational leaders embody the qualities they expect from their teams—demonstrating commitment, resilience, and a relentless pursuit of excellence.

Legacy of Impact: Becoming a Catalyst for Positive Change

Leaders who lead with purpose leave behind a legacy of impact. Their influence extends beyond profits to societal contributions, employee development, and a culture of ethical business practices.

leading with purpose transcends conventional leadership—it's a philosophy that embodies vision, values, and positive impact. Entrepreneurs who lead with purpose understand that their influence extends far beyond the confines of their business; it shapes the industry, fosters innovation, and leaves an indelible mark on the world. By nurturing empowered teams, upholding ethical standards, and embodying the qualities of an inspirational leader, entrepreneurs can illuminate a path that not only leads to business success but also creates a better future for all.

"Leadership is not about being in charge. It is about taking care of those in your charge." - **Simon Sine k**

Leading by Example
Modeling the Values of Your Company

In the intricate tapestry of leadership, one thread stands out prominently—leading by example. It's the art of embodying the values, principles, and behaviors that define a company's culture. Leading by example transcends rhetoric; it's a powerful demonstration that sets the tone for organizational dynamics, inspires trust, and shapes the conduct of employees. This chapter delves into the profound practice of leading by example—how it influences corporate identity, nurtures a cohesive team, and elevates the entire business ecosystem.

The Silent Influence: Unveiling the Impact of Modeling Values
Leading by example is a form of silent influence that resonates far beyond explicit directives. When leaders embody the values they espouse, employees are inspired to align their actions with those values, creating a ripple effect throughout the organization.

Cultural Integrity: Reinforcing Company Values
Values are the bedrock of corporate culture. Leaders who lead by example breathe life into these values, reinforcing their significance in daily operations and fostering an environment where employees instinctively embody them.

Trust in Action: Building Credibility and Loyalty
Trust is a currency of leadership. Leading by example establishes credibility by showcasing integrity, consistency, and authenticity. When employees witness leaders living the values, trust flourishes, and loyalty is cultivated.

Inspiring Commitment: Aligning Teams with a Shared Vision
When leaders practice what they preach, they align their teams with a shared vision. Leading by example demonstrates the dedication required to achieve organizational goals, motivating employees to invest their best efforts.

Conflict Resolution and Problem Solving: A Model for Behavior
In the face of challenges, leaders who lead by example model constructive conflict resolution and problem-solving. Their behavior becomes a

blueprint for handling adversity with grace, resilience, and a solutions-oriented mindset.

Employee Development: Nurturing Growth Through Mentorship

Leading by example extends to mentorship. When leaders demonstrate a commitment to personal and professional growth, they inspire employees to seek growth opportunities and take charge of their own development.

Influence Beyond the Organization: Impact on the Industry

Leaders who lead by example extend their influence beyond their company's walls. Their ethical conduct and principled behavior set standards for the industry, fostering a culture of responsible business practices.

leading by example is a beacon of leadership that transcends words. Entrepreneurs who understand the profound impact of modeling company values recognize that their behavior speaks volumes, resonating with employees, customers, and partners alike. By weaving the fabric of corporate culture with integrity, inspiring trust, and nurturing a sense of purpose, leaders who lead by example illuminate a path that not only guides their teams but also shapes the industry and creates a lasting legacy. "Leadership is not about being in the front; it is about taking others to the front." - John C. Maxwell

Empowering Your Team
Fostering a Collaborative Environment

In the intricate choreography of leadership, one of the most profound dances is that of empowerment. It's the art of nurturing a collaborative environment where each team member's potential is recognized, valued, and harnessed. Empowering your team transcends mere delegation; it's about cultivating a sense of ownership, encouraging innovation, and creating a space where every voice contributes to the symphony of success. This chapter delves into the transformative practice of empowering your team—how it nurtures creativity, boosts morale, and elevates the overall performance of your organization.

The Dynamic of Empowerment: Unveiling the Impact

Empowering your team is a dynamic that infuses a surge of energy into the workplace. It's an acknowledgment that each individual possesses unique talents and insights, and their contribution is essential for the collective achievement of organizational goals.

Ownership and Accountability: Fostering a Sense of Belonging

Empowerment rests on the pillars of ownership and accountability. When team members are empowered, they take ownership of their roles, become accountable for their actions, and align their efforts with the larger mission of the organization.

Cultivating Creativity: Nurturing a Culture of Innovation

Empowerment unleashes creativity. When team members are empowered to voice their ideas, take calculated risks, and contribute to problem-solving, they become catalysts for innovation that drives the organization forward.

Morale and Engagement: Elevating Employee Satisfaction

Empowerment is a morale booster. When team members feel trusted, valued, and empowered to make meaningful contributions, their job satisfaction soars, leading to higher engagement and reduced turnover.

Collaboration and Synergy: Forging a Unified Team

Empowerment fosters collaboration. When team members are empowered to share their perspectives and collaborate on projects, a sense of synergy emerges—a dynamic where diverse talents combine to produce remarkable results.

Mentorship and Growth: Navigating the Path of Development

Empowerment extends to mentorship. When leaders empower their teams, they provide guidance, offer opportunities for skill enhancement, and foster an environment where individuals can thrive and reach their full potential.

Impact on Organizational Culture: An Ecosystem of Empowerment

The practice of empowering your team becomes a cultural cornerstone. It shapes the way decisions are made, the way communication flows, and the way individuals at all levels are encouraged to contribute and lead.

In conclusion, empowering your team is a transformative leadership approach that nurtures a fertile ground for innovation, collaboration, and growth. Entrepreneurs who recognize the power of empowerment understand that their role is not just to lead but also to uplift, inspire, and amplify the collective potential of their team members. By fostering an environment of ownership, accountability, and mutual respect, leaders empower their teams to achieve greatness, elevate their contributions, and collectively compose a symphony of success.

"Leadership is not about being in control. It is about empowering others to be their best."

Giving Back
Incorporating Social Responsibility into Your Business

In the tapestry of modern business, a new thread is being woven—an unwavering commitment to social responsibility. Beyond the pursuit of profits, entrepreneurs are recognizing the profound impact their businesses can have on society. Incorporating social responsibility is not just a trend; it's a transformational shift that encompasses ethical practices, community engagement, and sustainable initiatives. This chapter delves into the compelling concept of giving back—how it shapes a business's identity, fosters goodwill, and creates a legacy of positive change.

The Purpose of Impact: Redefining Business Goals

Incorporating social responsibility transcends traditional business objectives. It's an awakening to the potential of businesses to be agents of positive change, leaving an indelible mark on communities and the environment.

Ethical Foundations: Aligning Business Practices with Values

Social responsibility is built upon ethical foundations. Entrepreneurs who incorporate this ethos prioritize fair labor practices, ethical sourcing, and transparency in their operations.

Community Engagement: Nurturing Local and Global Impact

Incorporating social responsibility involves active community engagement. Entrepreneurs can support local initiatives, contribute to social causes, and engage in philanthropic efforts that resonate with their company's values.

Environmental Stewardship: Embracing Sustainability

Sustainability is at the heart of social responsibility. Entrepreneurs who prioritize environmental stewardship adopt eco-friendly practices, reduce their carbon footprint, and champion initiatives that protect the planet.

Employee Empowerment: Fostering a Culture of Giving

Incorporating social responsibility extends to employees. Entrepreneurs can involve their teams in volunteering, charitable campaigns, and initiatives that allow employees to contribute to causes they care about.

Brand Reputation: Cultivating Trust and Goodwill

Incorporating social responsibility enhances brand reputation. Entrepreneurs who actively give back build trust with customers, partners, and stakeholders, elevating their brand's image and creating a loyal following.

Legacy of Impact: Building a Lasting Contribution

Incorporating social responsibility goes beyond short-term gains. Entrepreneurs leave a legacy of impact—a legacy that reflects their commitment to making the world a better place through responsible business practices.

In conclusion, incorporating social responsibility is a transformative journey that shapes the very essence of a business. Entrepreneurs who understand the power of giving back recognize that their actions reverberate beyond profits, influencing communities, inspiring change, and fostering a sense of purpose. By aligning business practices with ethical values, engaging with communities, and championing sustainability, entrepreneurs create a legacy that speaks to the heart of responsible entrepreneurship—a legacy that shines as a beacon of positive change in a complex world.

"The best way to find yourself is to lose yourself in the service of others."
- Mahatma Gandhi

Conclusion:

As we reach the conclusion of our journey through the pages of "From Startup to Success: The Entrepreneur's Guide," we stand at the threshold of possibilities. This book has been a compass, guiding you through the intricate landscapes of entrepreneurship—from planting the seed of an idea to cultivating a legacy of impact. The journey you've embarked upon is not merely about building a business; it's about crafting a narrative of resilience, innovation, and purpose.

You've explored the entrepreneurial spirit, delved into the power of vision, and defied limits in the pursuit of your dreams. You've embraced challenges, cultivated resilience, and learned from failures. You've empowered your team, fostered collaboration, and incorporated social responsibility into your business DNA. Every chapter has been a stepping stone, equipping you with insights, strategies, and the wisdom of leaders who have paved the way before you.

Remember that as an entrepreneur, you hold the power to shape your destiny and influence the world around you. The journey is not without its trials, but it's in those challenges that you'll find the opportunities for growth and transformation. The road to success is not a straight line; it's a tapestry woven with dedication, adaptability, and a relentless pursuit of excellence.

The pages of this book have provided you with a compass, but the true journey lies ahead—yours to explore, navigate, and conquer. As you venture forth, carry with you the lessons of entrepreneurship, the wisdom of leading with purpose, and the belief that every setback is a stepping stone to greatness. Let the powerful quotes, the practical advice, and the stories of visionaries be your guiding stars as you build, expand, and leave your mark on the world.

The path from startup to success is uniquely yours to forge. Embrace it with courage, resilience, and the unwavering commitment to creating not just a thriving business, but a legacy that resonates through time. As you continue on your journey, remember the words of Mark Twain: "The secret of getting ahead is getting started." Your journey has already begun—now, it's up to you to make it extraordinary.

With the knowledge gained from these pages and the fire of ambition burning within, you're equipped to not only navigate the challenges of entrepreneurship but to rise above them and thrive. As you continue to write the chapters of your own entrepreneurial story, may your journey be filled with purpose, growth, and the fulfillment of your greatest aspirations.

- The Ongoing Journey: Celebrating Milestones and Setting New Goals

As you reflect upon the journey outlined in "From Startup to Success: The Entrepreneur's Guide," remember that entrepreneurship is a continuous voyage of growth and evolution. Each milestone achieved is a testament to your dedication and vision. Celebrate these achievements, for they are the stepping stones that pave the way for even greater accomplishments. But also recognize that as one goal is met, new horizons emerge. Embrace the ongoing journey with enthusiasm, using the knowledge and inspiration gained from this guide to set new goals, navigate uncharted territories, and craft a narrative of innovation and impact that continues to inspire both yourself and those around you.

- Embracing the Unpredictable: Thriving in an Ever-Changing Business Landscape

In the intricate tapestry of entrepreneurship, adaptation is the thread that weaves success. The business world is a dynamic canvas where change is the constant brushstroke, reshaping markets, technologies, and consumer behaviors. Thriving amidst the unpredictable demands an agile mindset—a willingness to anticipate, innovate, and pivot. Entrepreneurs who embrace the fluidity of the business landscape, capitalize on disruptions as opportunities, and prioritize customer-centric strategies, not only survive but lead the charge in shaping the future. Resilience, agility, and a commitment to continuous learning are the compasses that navigate uncharted territories, enabling entrepreneurs to transform challenges into triumphs and evolve as industry pioneers.

- Your Legacy: Making a Lasting Impact as an Entrepreneurial Visionary

As the final stroke on the canvas of your entrepreneurial journey, legacy takes center stage. Beyond profits and milestones, your legacy is the impression you leave on the world—an embodiment of your values, your vision, and your impact. Your legacy is not a final destination, but a continuation—a testament to the dedication, innovation, and purpose you've woven into your business. As an entrepreneurial visionary, your legacy is the resonance of your influence, inspiring future generations to dare, dream, and create. It's the ripples you send forth into the fabric of time, an enduring mark that speaks to the transformative power of entrepreneurship and the indomitable spirit of those who forge their path.

Remember, this book is not just a guide; it's a roadmap to unleash the entrepreneur within you, guiding you from the inception of your startup to achieving remarkable success. Let these powerful words and quotes drive you as you embark on this transformative journey in the world of business.